Judy DuCharme

THE
CHEESEHEAD
DEVOTIONAL

Daily Meditations for Packer Fans

Kickoff Edition

THE CHEESEHEAD DEVOTIONAL: DAILY MEDITATIONS FOR GREEN BAY
PACKER FANS, KICKOFF EDITION
Published by Lighthouse Publishing of the Carolinas
2333 Barton Oaks Dr., Raleigh, NC, 27614

ISBN 978-1-938499-23-4
Copyright © 2012 by Judy DuCharme
Cover design by Wisdom House Books: www.wisdomhousebooks.com
Book design by Reality Info Systems www.realityinfo.com

Available in print from your local bookstore, online, or from the publisher at: www.
lighthousepublishingofthecarolinas.com

For more information on this book and the author visit:
www.packerdigest.com

Library of Congress Cataloging-in-Publication Data
DuCharme, Judy.
The Cheesehead Devotional, Kickoff Edition / Judy DuCharme 1st ed.

Printed in the United States of America

Praise for
The Cheesehead Devotional

I pastored in Green Bay from 1992 to 2005. During that time many of the Packer players attended our church, Bayside Christian Fellowship - Reggie White, Bryce Paup, and Ray Nitschke, to name a few. As a former Packer chaplain I am certain you will love this little book. Judy has captured the true heart of a Christian Packer fan!

~ Rev. Arni Jacobson

I have always believed the Packers were religion in these parts. Judy's correlation of Packers history and our team's accomplishments tied to scriptural passages and spiritual messages bring that belief to life.

~ Wayne Larrivee
American sportscaster and play-by-play announcer for the
Green Bay Packers

As a long-time, long-distance Packers fan who recently retired to Door County Wisconsin, this devotional brought back some wonderful memories of the great Packers games we enjoyed watching. But even more important are the Biblical references that relate to our Packers' exploits that point us to praise and worship of the King of Kings and Lord of Lords, Jesus Christ! Thanks, Judy DuCharme!

Faith Connor Murray

The Cheesehead Devotional is an extraordinarily entertaining read that not only captures, up-close and personal, the character of our beloved Packers, but also expresses the sentiments of believers on all sports teams. Love it!

Robert Woolverton Murray
Author of Poems for Faith, Arabian Sketches,
Finding I AM

Table of Contents

Foreword

From the time I received Judy's devotional until right up to this moment, I could have used each daily extra point. I have been dealing with my elderly parents' major health issues. My Dad is still in ICU with blood on his brain. Each day, I just rub his head and pray hoping to bring comfort to him and myself.

The Cheesehead Devotional is a great adventure for those who may not pick up a Bible for guidance. It is also a great reference for those would read the Bible in conjunction with this devotional. Reggie loved to read the Word of God. He was so inspired by it. Our daily routine became more about the Word than about anything else. When he retired, he indulged himself in the Torah. It brought him so close to his Hebraic roots. It is there we found the most peace. Our heritage; our history; idioms we never understood.

Some Packer fans who have watched Reggie from afar only knew him as a kind, gentle football player that broke records and did his job well. Those who heard him speak on a personal level knew him as the wonderful husband, father, and Servant of our FATHER of Abraham, Isaac and Jacob.

I congratulate Judy for putting some flavor into a devotional that could become a playbook for some, a reference for others, and a life-changing experience for those who choose to go deeper.

Sara White,
#92 ½, wife of the late Reggie White, #92

Speak God's Word

1 Peter 4:8-11

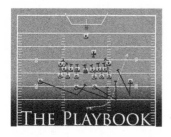

FROM THE PLAYBOOK:

If anyone speaks, they should do so as one who speaks the very words of God.

1 Peter 4:11 (NIV)

"**R**eggie, this is God. Come to Green Bay."

Defensive End Reggie White needed to decide which team to join in 1993. Mike Holmgren didn't realize he talked like God, but he knew Reggie wanted God's will more than a lucrative contract.

After Reggie "The Minister of Defense" White came to Green Bay, he liked to tell the story of Mike Holmgren's phone call.[1] It was very funny, and God used it. Reggie helped the Packers become a strong team that would win Super Bowl XXXI.

Reggie knew his strength came from the Lord. He led the locker room in prayer. He led the players of both teams in prayer after most games in the middle of the field. Reggie was an amazing man, and Packer fans might not have known that if Mike Holmgren had not stepped out and spoken like God.

Speaking like God is what all of us are called to do. In 2 Corinthians 4:13, Paul wrote "I believe, therefore I speak."

Our words carry great authority. Proverbs 18:21 says, "Life

and death are in the power of the tongue."

God's words bring life. They bring the Holy Spirit into a situation. When we use God's words to bless others, those words carry good. If we use words carelessly, they can injure the mind, will, and emotions. Learn to speak God's Word to yourself and others to share the blessings of God.

If speaking like God is new to you, start by reading Psalms and Proverbs. Follow the example in Proverbs 3:4 and say, "Self, this is God. Trust in the Lord with all your heart, and He will direct your paths."

Learn God's Word and speak boldly.

Extra Point:

Lord, help me to immerse myself in Your Word and speak boldly as I share it with others. Amen.

Fix the Typos!

Ephesians 4:25-32

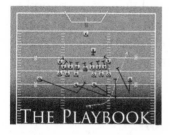

FROM THE PLAYBOOK:

Do not let any unwholesome talk come out of your mouths, but only what is helpful for building others up according to their needs, that it may benefit those who listen.

Ephesians 4:29 (NIV)

Driving to church, I glanced at the sign. It said, "Go Bears. Beat Da Packers." I immediately knew my mission. Before I got the coffee ready or made sure the Pastor had water at the pulpit, I found the phone number of the sign owners.

"Joy, I just went by the sign. It doesn't say, 'Go Packers. Beat Da Bears.' It says, 'Go Bears. Beat Da Packers!'"

She gasped. "We haven't been out yet. We'll get right over there."

We laughed, but we knew it was serious business for Packers fans. The sign had to be changed back quickly. It was the day of the NFC Championship game between the Chicago Bears and the Green Bay Packers, division rivals for eighty-nine years. Most jawing between fans is good-natured, but the loyalty is serious. Bears fans everywhere would delight in those words.

Do your words sometimes say the opposite of what you mean? The enemy of your soul comes to steal, kill, and destroy.

He delights in persuading others to misinterpret your words. Sometimes the problem isn't as easy to fix as a few letters on a sign, and it isn't as funny.

The Bible says the tongue is a small body part, but like a rudder, it steers a very big ship. Like a sign, your words carry strong sentiments. They can be powerful messages for good or evil. The messages you send are like signs by the road for all to see, so set a guard on your mouth. Your words can deliver life or death—even typos. Choose life and fix the typos.

EXTRA POINT:

Lord, help me guard my words, and help my words bring life.

Praise Him!

Psalm 145:1-13

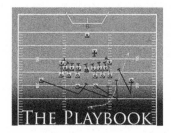

FROM THE PLAYBOOK:

Men shall speak of the might of Your awesome acts, and I will declare Your greatness.

Psalm 145:6

"To God be the Glory! To God be the Glory!" Packer Wide Receiver Greg Jennings jumped up and down, ecstatic, after winning Super Bowl XLV. Packer fans everywhere jumped with him.

"This is an answer to prayer," he said to Pam Oliver, Fox Sports reporter, at the end of the game.[2] Greg gave God praise and thanks before anyone else.

He knew God was the source of all blessings. Without God's grace, all the hard work, blood, sweat, tears, and perseverance could not bring the sweet victory he experienced. Greg believed God built the Packer team to win and all of their work was blessed by God.

In a previous statement, Greg quoted Luke 12:48 saying, "To whom much is given, much is required."[3] As the recipient of athletic talent and a national platform, number eighty-five determined to honor God and felt it was his responsibility to praise the Lord.

Praise can bring God on the scene because He likes to be

where praise is. Greg Jennings didn't wait until he was a Super Bowl champion to give God praise. He made a practice of praising God every step of the way. It wasn't always easy, but he practiced it like he practiced running his routes.

Is that our first response when we are blessed? Is that our response before we're blessed? We may work hard, but God is the one we should credit first, no matter what.

When we give credit to God, we'll have many more opportunities to give Him thanks.

EXTRA POINT:

Lord, help me to praise and honor You in every situation.

Memories

1 Chronicles 16:7-36

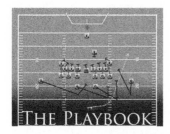

FROM THE PLAYBOOK:

Remember His marvelous works which He has done, His wonders and the judgments of His mouth.

1 Chronicles 16:12

1962. The last time the Green Bay Packers started a season 10-0. That winning streak ended on Thanksgiving Day against the Detroit Lions. At halftime, the Lions were ahead 23-0 and won the game 26-14. Bart Starr and Vince Lombardi were no longer undefeated.

That day was a terrific day for the Lions, who had been in second place behind the Packers. It was like the Lion's Super Bowl. Jerry Kramer, Packers' starting right guard in 1962, said, "They ought to give them a ring or something for it, have a holiday or something because it's a highlight in their history."[4] Bart Starr, famed quarterback for the Packers, got sacked eleven times. The Packers earned only 122 yards of offense. Lions' Linebacker Joe Schmidt said his team, at that time, was out to prove to the world they were as good as or better than Green Bay. The Lions finished the season 11-3, while the Packers were 14-1.

The comparisons to that 1962 season were everywhere

preceding the 2011 Thanksgiving Day game. The Lions hoped to repeat history.

However, the Packers shut down Lions Receiver Calvin Johnson, the man who turned many Lions games into victories with his superior play. Even missing three injured starters, the Packer defense showed one of their best games. Ryan Pickett tipped a pass from Lions Quarterback Matt Stafford. Linebacker Clay Matthews made a great grab for an interception. The Packers won 27-15, almost an exact flip-flop of the 1962 score.

Historical reruns can make for a great conversation and story. However, in our minds and spirits, they can sometimes be more detrimental than good. It is so easy to fall into the mindset that because a situation went a certain way once, it more than likely will go that way again. It can be a defeatist mentality if the event was negative and can be an unsupported hope if one simply assumes history will repeat itself in the positive events.

The Bible warns us against this type of thinking when it tells us to forget what lies behind and press on to what is ahead. We are told to remember the good things God has done and put our faith in Him, not in repeating history by fate. Faith and fate are not the same. Faith has eyes that look ahead, hearts that believe God's promises, minds that make right choices, feet that diligently move forward in obedience, and hands that work hard.

History is great for reminiscing, enjoying, and making future plans, but trusting fate will leave you in the dust, while faith in God will take you to new heights.

EXTRA POINT:

God, I put my trust and faith in You no matter what has or has not happened in my past. I expect great things ahead, because You are a marvelous God.

Discipline Has Its Reward

1 Corinthians 9:24-27

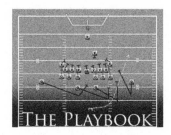

FROM THE PLAYBOOK:

"I discipline my body and bring it into subjection, lest, when I have preached to others, I myself should become disqualified."

1 Corinthians 9:27

One step. Sometimes that's all it takes to miss a ball or make a sensational play. There's very little room for error.

Cornerback Tramon Williams delighted us with an interception from Brett Favre when Green Bay played Minnesota in 2010. Brett's popularity in Green Bay hit an all-time low when he decided to wear that purple uniform and play for the team most disliked by Packer fans. We tolerated him playing for the Jets, but the Vikings!?

In that game, Tramon played man-to-man coverage and knew the line-up was for a pass. He watched Brett and recalled film on this exact play. Brett looked at the receiver to Tramon's left and forward. Because he was in man-to-man and not zone, Tramon couldn't go there. He stayed with his man, but because of his experience and film study, he didn't believe Brett's eyes. Sure enough, the ball came like a bullet for Tramon's man, and

Tramon was positioned to make the interception. [5]

Discipline is the most important aspect of playing football. Do your job. Obey the direction given in the huddle. Run your route. Study film. Pay attention. Focus.

How's your focus? It can be improved by studying the Bible. We can study how to walk in love, forgive, be responsible, and be truthful. We can study how Jesus lived and reacted. We can practice doing what is right and meditate on the truth of God's Word. We can be disciplined so when an opportunity comes to be offended, we forgive instead.

To be in the right place to help those around us win, we must pay attention to our hearts—hearts that have been disciplined by the Bible.

EXTRA POINT:

Lord, I commit myself to You, and I determine to discipline myself according to the Bible so I can do what is right.

Are You Ready for a Miracle?

Psalm 126:1-6

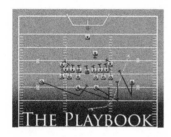

FROM THE PLAYBOOK:

The Lord has done great things for us, and we are glad.

Psalm 126:3

I love football miracles. I scream and jump with everyone else when they happen. The Packer-Viking game in November of 2000 was no exception. And I was there.

It was overtime, tied 20-20. Brett passed, and Wide Receiver Antonio Freeman went up, missed it, and fell on the ground. The amazing opportunity to win appeared lost. I watched from the southeast corner of the end zone. Freeman lay on the 15-yard line closest to the southwest corner of the end zone. All of a sudden he jumped up and ran into the end zone with the football!

How did he do that? The crowd was deafening, and the surprise all encompassing.

Viking player, Chris Dishman, thought the ball was dead. He stopped and agonized over missing a great interception. In reality, the ball bounced on the back of Freeman's left shoulder and into his hand as he rolled over. Then, to everyone's amazement and with no one trying to stop him, Antonio Freeman scored six for the Green Bay Packers, punctuating the win with a Lambeau Leap.

Things can change quickly in a football game. Do you expect sudden changes for good in life or only changes for the bad?

Sometimes we fall down and think, "That's it. I've lost the game." Then, before we know it, we find ourselves in the end zone making a Lambeau Leap.

Every football player has dreams of being the one to make that amazing play to win the game. What if Freeman never had those dreams? What if he pounded the ground or closed his eyes in defeat? He wouldn't be known for making one of the greatest receptions of all time.

When loss seems inevitable, tune in for the possibility of a miracle.

EXTRA POINT:

Lord, today I choose to look for the possibility of a miracle rather than defeat.

Mr. Rodger's Neighborhood

Psalm 5

FROM THE PLAYBOOK:

For You, O Lord, will bless the righteous; With favor You will surround him as with a shield.

Psalm 5:12

"Hello boys and girls. Can you say 'twelve and zero'? I thought you could." It was the *New Mr. Rodger's Neighborhood.* Using a picture of Mr. Rogers clad in his everyday sweater and soft cloth tennis shoes, the head of Packer quarterback Aaron Rodgers smiled enigmatically. You could almost hear that kind, soothing voice that talked to children all over the world for so many years on the television program *Mr. Roger's Neighborhood.*[6]

12-0. It had never happened in Packer history. The Super Bowl Packers played a perfect season, so far. It had been really fun. They were led by that calm, capable quarterback, Aaron Rodgers, who was setting all kinds of records on his way to being the NFL's Most Valuable Player.

Kurt Warner, owner of two MVP awards himself, called Aaron Rodgers a prototypical quarterback. "If you were designing a quarterback . . . you'd build it just like that."[7] When Aaron accepted the award at the NFL Honors, we all knew he'd rather be preparing for the Super Bowl. Yet, he accepted graciously and humbly.

His quarterback rating for the season was 122.5. His yards-per-pass average was 9.2. He had forty-five touchdown receptions with only six interceptions, and his team went 15-1.[8] The records go on and on.

Rodgers is also one of the best photobombers on the team. Every week, captains are chosen for the game. It is an honor and pictures are taken. In almost every picture, Rodgers is seen behind the captains, blowing a horn, giving rabbit ears, or making a funny face.

When asked the best part of his position, he said it's being a leader. He told his mom he no longer wanted to be one of the best players in football, he wanted to be the best man in football.[9] Wow.

However, he knows he is part of the team and honors their support. In the Detroit game on Thanksgiving Day, November 24, 2011, Rodgers decided to run. It was third down and we badly needed a first down. No one was open and Rodgers took off.

Kuhn saw a Lion getting ready to take out his quarterback. Kuhn sailed across the field laterally and, with emphasis, took out the Detroit player. Rodgers made the first down, and not long after, the Packers scored.[10] In watching the replay, Rodgers may well have cried "Kuuuuuuhn" as all the fans do when Kuhn makes one of his many great plays.

Are you the star on your team? Whether you're the star or not, you are on the team and it live or dies with you. Rodgers is a perfectionist and gets after himself for not throwing a perfect ball, but he knows the perfect ball doesn't arrive if receivers don't run their routes and the front line doesn't keep him clean.

Rodgers has learned to depend on his team as well as lead them. What a skill!

Most of us won't find ourselves on the same stage that Aaron Rodgers is on, but we are placed where we can have strong influence, leadership, and teamwork. Are you willing to work to be the best member on your team, to work to be the best person in life that you can be? It is all a part of knowing and serving the Lord. He tells us, "Whatever your hand finds to do, do it with all your might." If we fulfill that one verse, what a changed world we would see.

EXTRA POINT:

Lord, thank You that I can be the best me possible.

Rewards of Consistency

Ephesians 6: 10-18

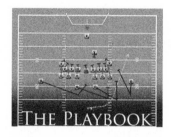

FROM THE PLAYBOOK:

Be strong in the Lord and the power of His might.

Ephesians 6:10

Consistency. That was one thing Brett Favre had. He played 275 games in a row for Green Bay, including the playoffs.[11] He played through pain and injury. He played no matter what. He loved the game of football like few we've ever seen.

While many teams frequently change quarterbacks, Green Bay had one quarterback for sixteen years who never missed a game.

It isn't easy to play football. Brett didn't always have an easy time, especially when he threw interceptions, and even more so when an interception caused a loss. One of the biggest losses happened in the championship playoff game with the New York Giants at the end of the 2008 season. The previous week, the Packers easily defeated Seattle in a home game snowstorm. We knew then we were on our way to the Super Bowl. The Giants game was at home in January, and we knew we couldn't lose.

However, we didn't plan on the temperature being thirty-five degrees below zero. Brett's performance, though marvelous in the cold in his early years, began to sink with the low temperatures.

The game was close. We could win. Down to the last play, it seemed easy. We celebrated. Brett could pull it off. He always did. Then our hearts stopped. Interception! It wasn't just another loss. This loss meant no Super Bowl. Who knew if Brett would have another opportunity to get to the Super Bowl? We grieved for him—and for ourselves.

Still, Brett was consistent. Consistent to be there for the next game, the next practice, the next meeting. He refused to give up. Often, he took too much responsibility, but he never gave up trying to win the game. We appreciated that.

Can it be said of you that you never quit? Do you love what you do and who you are?

The Bible tells us what our priorities should be: to love the Lord our God with all our heart, soul, and strength.

Is your passion visible to all who observe you? You may not have the audience Brett Favre had, but you are seen by an audience. Be consistent to keep going, loving, and giving with all that is in you.

Extra Point:

Lord, I desire to be strong and consistent and do great things for You. Amen.

Embrace Joy

Psalm 16:5-11

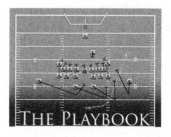

FROM THE PLAYBOOK:

"In Your presence is fullness of joy. At Your right hand are pleasures forevermore."

Psalm 16:11

Do screaming Packer fans and coyotes really sound alike?

It was Super Bowl XLV, and friends were watching the game with us. At one point, our friend ran out to get something he forgot in the car.

While he was gone, Ben Roethlisberger passed the ball for a certain first down. Nick Collins darted in front of the receiver to intercept and run the ball back for a Packer touchdown. We ran those thirty yards with him, jumping and squealing all the way. Our friend thought our shouts were the cries of the coyotes in the woods near our home.

The word fan is short for fanatic. Most Packer fans have no trouble being fanatics. We love our team, and whether we're by ourselves or with thousands of other fans, we squeal and shriek and yell and jump. We consider it normal.

Are you a fan of God? Have you ever been called a religious fanatic? Would you be offended by that? Calling someone a fanatic means they are extremely demonstrative in their loyalties. Does that apply to your faith?

Why not sing and shout and dance for God like we do for the Packers? Why not wear our love for Him on our sleeve as quickly as we don our green and gold. We love our Packers, but when it comes down to it, our faith and our trust in God will be more important than our loyalty to any team.

Who says we can't enjoy God as much and more than a Packer win? In Him is fullness of joy and unending pleasure. I Timothy 6:17 says God richly gives us all things to enjoy. He intended for joy to be an important part of life. What great and amazing joy is available in God!

EXTRA POINT:

If you get to know the Lord, you'll find you can enjoy Him above all else.

The Path of Pursuit

Psalm 23:1-6

FROM THE PLAYBOOK:

"Surely Your goodness and unfailing love will pursue me all the days of my life, and I will live in the house of the Lord forever."

Psalm 23:6 (NLT)

One day, I was chasing down Ray Nitschke, linebacker for the 1960s Green Bay Packers. Would I catch him in time? Should I tackle him?

On our way to a game at Lambeau Field, we went to church in Green Bay. We arrived as the early service released. Our son's friend was so excited to see the great Packer player chatting in the lobby. Mr. Nitschke graciously autographed the boy's church bulletin.

We happily proceeded to our seats when our young friend realized Nitschke inadvertently gave him a card with the autographed bulletin. Knowing Nitschke's wife had recently passed away, I was sure it was a sympathy card. I took the card and hurried back to the lobby. Nitschke was in the parking lot. I began running to catch him before he drove away. What a feeling to be chasing down the great Ray Nitschke. I caught him right before he got into his car. I didn't tackle him, but I really felt like a Packer player in that moment.

Pursuit is an interesting thing. Do we need it to go where God wants us? Scripture tells us we do. Matthew 6:33 tells us to seek first, to pursue, God's righteousness and all that is necessary will be provided us.

What are you pursuing? Is good pursuing you? In a football game, the player pursues the football and opposing players at all costs. It is the best means of winning the game. Without pursuit, the game is lost and usually boring.

When we begin to truly pursue God and His purposes for us, we usually find good pursuing us.

EXTRA POINT:

Lord, I pursue You with my whole heart. I thank You that you have pursued me with Your love.

His Love is Great

Psalm 103:10-22

FROM THE PLAYBOOK:

Just as a father has compassion on his children, so the Lord has compassion on those who fear Him.

Psalm 103:13 (NASB)

We watched with tears in our eyes and our hearts in our hands as Brett Favre took the field the day after his father died. How could he do it? Should he do it? We knew his love for his team and his family. All of us, like Brett, could hear his dad say, "Get out there, Brett, and win this game."

The loss of a father strikes deep within us. When my dad passed, I was amazed at the depth of my grief. He lived a full life and died at age seventy-eight. I only saw him two or three times a year because I lived in a different state, but I wept for hours, for days. He was a good, kind man.

I think everyone who has lost a parent relived that grief with Brett. What a most inopportune time—a Monday night play-off game with the whole world watching. His teammates vowed to catch everything he threw, and they did.

Brett felt his dad had a hand in all those great plays.[12] He had the best game of his career that night. He completed twenty-two of thirty passes for 399 yards with four touchdowns and a resounding win over Oakland, finishing the game 41-7.

God's care for us is great. God knows loss and grief. His Son died on a bigger stage than a Monday night football game. The ultimate result of Christ's crucifixion was an exciting and amazing win for all creation.

Jesus won over death, sickness, depression, fear, and loneliness. He isn't with us for just one game. He is with us every moment, giving us direction, wisdom, and joy. We can take His victory and rejoice. Because of the death of Jesus, we win.

EXTRA POINT:

Thank You, Lord, that You won the victory for me.

Keep Going

Romans 8:31-39

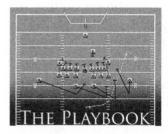

FROM THE PLAYBOOK:

Yet in all these things we are more than conquerors through Him who loved us.

Romans 8:37

Jermichael Finley was out for the season. The Packers played their fifth game of the 2010 season against the Washington Redskins. Only fourteen minutes into the game, the Packers were second-and-two at the 16-yard line. Rodgers faked a hand-off, rolled to the left and threw an easy pass to Donald Lee. Landry of the Redskins grabbed Lee's arm, causing a fumble that Kareem Moore picked up. Moore headed for the end zone. Tight End Finley tackled Moore and didn't get up. Although it looked like a minor injury, he left the game on a cart with a torn meniscus in his right knee, ending his season.[13]

A stand-out tight end, Finley was considered a key player for getting the Packers to the Super Bowl. Losing him was devastating for fans and players alike.

Then things got worse. Donald Lee sprained his chest, and by the end of the game, eight players were hurt. Injury after injury seemed to be knocking the Packers off the Super Bowl ladder, rung by rung.

Despite being prone to injury, the Packers were not prone

to depression. They had depth of position. The backups were prepared to play, and the Packers kept going with their vision of victory before them. They kept playing well and winning. Their losses were never by more than four points, and they never trailed more than seven points in any game.

Peaking at the end of the regular season by beating the Giants and the Bears, they went into the wildcard game at Philadelphia with high hopes. The Packer defense contained Michael Vick and then picked him off in the end zone with thirty-three seconds left. The Packers won 21-16.[14] Could they go to Atlanta and beat the first seed Falcons?

They won with a resounding score of 48-21. Plus, what could be better than facing their division rivals, the Chicago Bears, in the game to determine who would go to the Super Bowl? Who can forget Raji running in that interception for a touchdown? It wasn't a pretty game, but the final score was beautiful: 21-14.

The Packers headed to the Super Bowl with a team not only prone to injury, but also prone to win—no matter what.

Everyone said the Pittsburgh Steelers were more seasoned and, therefore, more likely to win. Most of Pittsburgh's players had been to more than one Super Bowl, whereas Chad Clifton and Charles Woodson were the only Super Bowl veterans from the Packers.[15] However, a season of injuries and media scrutiny over Rodgers replacing Favre provided plenty of adversity training for the Packers. The Packers were hungry for a win, and they knew this was their time.

What is it that seems impossible to you right now? What is it that you were excited about, only to have complications arise and threaten your success? Can you keep your eye on the plan God gave you and the fire of His Spirit in your own spirit?

Why decide that you can't accomplish your goal because of life's setbacks?

Philippians 3 tells us to keep our eyes on the goal—the high calling of Christ. That high calling is what He puts in your heart to serve Him and glorify Him. He says we are more than conquerors, so don't merely survive after a setback. Move forward and be all that God has made you to be. It may not be easy, but if you persevere, you'll reach your destination.

EXTRA POINT:

Lord, help me know that no matter what, with You on my side, I am more than a conqueror.

Join the Circle

1 Timothy 2:1-8

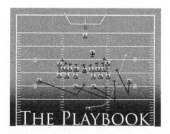

FROM THE PLAYBOOK:

I will therefore that men pray everywhere, lifting up holy hands, without wrath and doubting.

1 Timothy 2:8 (KJV)

I could never leave a game until I saw the circle—players kneeling and praying. One of the highlights of hanging around after games at Lambeau was seeing the players from both teams huddled at the 50-yard line for prayer. What a statement! Win or lose, they prayed.

In the movie, *Facing the Giants*, the coach told his players, "If we win, we praise Him, and if we lose, we praise Him."[16] That's what the Packers and their opponents did.

It brought joy to my heart. I had no doubt that it brought joy to God's heart as well.

The Bible reminds us, "Whatever you do, do it all to the glory of God." The Packers had a lot of players who did just that: Reggie White, Robert Brooks, Ken Reutgers, John Michaels, and Bryce Paup, to name a few.

Imagine if, at the end of your work day, you and all your coworkers met in the lobby of your workplace and knelt or held hands and prayed. Imagine if this happened in courthouses, stores, schools, and offices around your city or hometown.

Would it make a difference? I think it would. Increased productivity? Increased commitment? Increased energy? Increased assistance? Increased right living?

What if two of you prayed? That would be a significant start.

Why not let the Packer prayer become an inspiration to start a prayer time with your colleagues? It may have an impact far beyond what you can imagine.

EXTRA POINT:

Lord, help me be an instrument of prayer and inspiration in my place of work.

When Time is Short

2 Corinthians 2:14-3:11

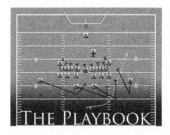

FROM THE PLAYBOOK:

Now thanks be to God who always leads us in triumph in Christ.

2 Corinthians 2:14

It was fourth down and one yard to go with twelve seconds left in the game and no time-outs. The Packers were behind Minnesota 20-16. Everyone was on their feet. We were in the twelfth row, corner of the end zone, on a Sunday afternoon in September 1999.

Brett Favre and the team lined up on the 23-yard line right in front of us. Everyone screamed. I prayed at the top of my lungs, but only God could hear me. I couldn't even hear myself. It was incredibly loud.

Brett snapped the ball. He couldn't spike it, and he couldn't call a timeout. He hadn't even called a play. He pump-faked to Schroeder and then threw to the end zone, and Corey Bradford arrived right in front of us to catch it. We won! Fourth-and-one, no time-outs, twelve seconds left, and we won! Then it *really* got loud.

We high-fived, hugged, and jumped up and down where there wasn't room to do so. It was marvelous. Later, Coach Ray Rhodes said, "That was close to a miracle, if not a miracle."[17] We were eye-witnesses!

I wonder if that's what it will be like in heaven when God hands out His rewards. We'll cheer for every teammate who gets his name called. We'll stomp and whistle for the win that lasts for eternity.

Will we get to cheer for you? I want to. God wants you there. If you never have, will you ask Him to be your Lord and Savior this moment, as if you only had twelve seconds left in your life? He'll make you a winner in life. He's passing the ball to you right now. Receive it. Receive Him. Receive salvation and truly live.

EXTRA POINT:

Lord, I receive You right now as Lord and Savior. Thank You for making me a winner in life.

One Thing

Philippians 3:7-16

FROM THE PLAYBOOK:

But one thing I do, forgetting those things which are behind and reaching forward to those things which are ahead.

Philippians 3:13

Bling! Bling! Bling! The Super Bowl LXV ring with a diamond-studded G was big and beautiful and well deserved. Did you see Donald Driver's picture with that ring? He smiled even bigger than he usually did.

The Super Bowl was Driver's game. Everyone wanted him to win a Super Bowl. As one of the most consistent, most likeable players in the NFL, it seemed he deserved it, though he had not been to one yet. In person, Driver was kind and generous. On the field, he was driven and disciplined.

The Super Bowl came on February 6, 2011. Driver's injury occurred at the end of the second quarter. The ball came hard and fast—a bullet. Driver made the dive, up and out, without caution for himself. His ankle twisted in the landing. He limped off the field while all of Packer Land groaned.

Driver spent half time getting it treated. He was determined to go back into the game. He'd waited all his life for this game and sitting on the sideline was not his plan. He determined he could do it. He would play through the pain. He pled with the trainers, and then fellow Wide Receiver Greg Jennings told him to jump. Total pain. Inability. No more game time. Sidelined.

Ever been sidelined? So much to give but sidelined? So much determination, yet you can't use it? What to do? Driver cheered his team on and noticed things to help his teammates do better. I wouldn't be surprised if he prayed, too. He stayed part of the team, and his teammates determined to pick up the slack. Nothing would deter them.[18]

Now Donald has the prize—a diamond and gold Super Bowl ring that is his forever. The Bible tells us that we have a prize. It's the high calling of God. A Super Bowl win is a high calling and an amazing prize, but the high calling of God is to know and accomplish the purposes and plans He designed for you.

Think of it! First, God planned a plan just for you. Not only that, He designed you to fit His plan. Right now He's engineering your days so you can fulfill the plan. And, just like the Packers, He's surrounded you with teammates who will help you get there and step in for you if you get knocked down. Rather ingenious, don't you think?

It is never too late to get in God's game. He has a roster spot selected for you.

Extra Point:

Thank You, Lord, that with Your help I will continue and receive the prize for the high calling You have given me.

Give It Your All

2 Timothy 2:1-10

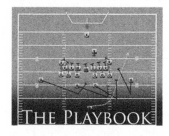

FROM THE PLAYBOOK:

You therefore must endure hardship, as a good soldier of Jesus Christ.

2 Timothy 2:3

"The ball's coming hard, going to break some of your fingers, just got to take it and wait for warm days."[19] James Jones, wide receiver, is matter of fact about playing in the cold. It's not the only tough thing he's faced. He spent some of his childhood in a homeless shelter.

Now, number eighty-nine and his wife have a program called "Love Jones for Kids." They provide eighty-nine wishes for homeless kids each year.

Toughness is a great quality in football and in life. Sometimes you drop the ball. James Jones knows that too well and has often been maligned by fans for drops that occurred at important turning points in the game. He admits that he spends more time looking at those bad plays than good ones, because they just make him mad.

Jones has a lot of good ones under his belt too. In the last game of the 2011 season against the Detroit Lions at Lambeau, Matt Flynn was quarterbacking to give Rodgers a rest. While they were in the huddle, Jones kept telling Matt to go deep on

Lions number twenty-three because he kept backing up and playing inside. It was the fourth quarter. The Packers were on the 46-yard line. Jones lined up right. Matt called a slant route in the huddle, but on the line he changed it to "all go" due to the coverage he saw. All go means straight out. Jones gave a little move to the inside and Matt drew him down with his eyes, throwing the Detroit cornerback off. Jones raced downfield, catching the ball on the 9-yard line and going out of bounds at the six. That forty-yard play resulted in the go-ahead touchdown two plays later.

Perhaps that catch resulted in a broken finger, but it didn't matter to Jones. He was there to help the team. He wanted the rest of the wide receivers, a tight bunch, to be proud of him. He wanted his two-month-old son to see him play well. As a Christian, he wanted to glorify his Lord by doing his best with all his might.

When we do our best for our team, our family, our core group of friends, and our Lord, we may take some hits, get some broken fingers. But as James Jones said, "You just take it and wait for warmer days." The Lord has many warmer days when the ball doesn't hit so hard and the tasks set before us are joyful and fun. Let's remember to not fear the tougher days because we have a big God who can take us from homelessness to providing a way out for others who have been where we were.

Extra Point:

Thank You, Lord, that You are the God who heals broken fingers and broken hearts with Your great love which You have so abundantly given to us.

Let Worship Roll

Colossians 3:12-17

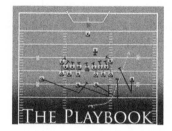

FROM THE PLAYBOOK:

Let the Word of Christ dwell in you richly in all wisdom, teaching and admonishing one another in psalms and hymns and spiritual songs, singing with grace in your hearts to the Lord.

Colossians 3:16

Dun-Ta-Dun-Dah. That music always brings an element of excitement. Football follows that music. It may be a game or sports coverage of players and events, but the music means football. For Packer fans, it's a rallying cry, a time to focus, a time to get ready.

When we love something, the music that goes with it triggers our emotions. At times, it actually places our memories with a specific event and we relive it every time we hear the music play. When it is a positive event, the emotions are amazing.

I enjoy hearing the music that brings my focus to football. I also find the most important music that courses through my being is worship music, music that honors God and lifts up His words within me.

What do you listen to? Do the songs that dwell in your mind and heart promote the goodness of God? Just as positive music can evoke positive emotions, negative music can evoke negative emotions. Have you ever noticed that with only a few notes, you can remember words to a song that you haven't thought of in years? Our soul stores words. Music provides a wonderful package in which to store them.

What you listen to over and over becomes imbedded into your subconscious thinking. It influences what you say and how you think. Wouldn't it be great if the words of God would spring into your mind, providing direction when you are faced with important and daily decisions? It will happen more and more when you study, memorize, and listen to the Bible and add worship songs to your music list.

Extra Point:

Lord, may Your Word and Your songs dwell richly in me.

Notice Your Turn-Arounds

Psalm 27:1-14

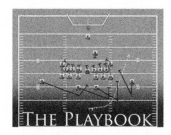

FROM THE PLAYBOOK:

"I would have lost heart, unless I had believed that I would see the goodness of the Lord in the land of the living."

Psalm 27:13

"Dear Jesus, please heal Reggie White's hamstring. We need him in the game." Taking my walk down the winding, tree-lined road, I often prayed, and I often prayed for the Packers. I echoed the prayer of many Packer fans that day.

It began at the Cincinnati Bengals game in December of 1995. There were less than seven minutes to play. The score was 17-10 Bengals. The offensive tackle dove for Reggie who jumped high to avoid a cut block. He heard a loud pop near his left knee and felt a cramping pain. Bengals Quarterback Jeff Black threw a pass as he rolled out. It went straight into Packer Safety Leroy Butler's hands.

Reggie needed help to get off the field and knew his season might be over. The hamstring had detached from the back of his knee and bunched up in the thigh. It removed his ability to push off and run.

Reggie missed the Tampa game the following week, which

ended his 166 game streak and the Packers lost. The doctor scheduled surgery. Disappointment descended on Packer fans.

About 9:30 the night before the next game, Reggie went to Mike Holmgren's home. As soon as Mike opened the door, Reggie burst out, "I'm healed. I'm playing."[20]

The next day news stations interrupted daytime programs to say Reggie had a miracle healing and would be playing. Fans and teammates were delighted. Some people actually decided to give their lives to God because of Reggie's healing. When his back-up found out Reggie was going to play, he said, "Man, I've gotta start reading the Bible more! That clean living must be doing it for you!"[21]

Your turn-arounds might not be as publicized as Reggie's, but your experiences can have a powerful effect on your colleagues, neighbors, friends, and families. When bad things happen, maybe it's an opportunity for God's amazing turn-around in your life.

Reggie was quick to believe, trust, and praise God. Your faith, attitude, persistence, and peace have an effect on those around you. Can you emulate Reggie's trust and confidence to stand firm on God's promises?

EXTRA POINT:

Lord, I will trust firmly in Your promises and believe You to work out things that seem impossible to me.

What's the Question?

2 Timothy 3:14 – 4:2

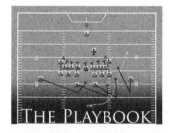

Preach the Word. Be ready in season and out of season. Convince, rebuke, exhort with all longsuffering and teaching.

2 Timothy 4:2

"Do you have faith in God?" my son Chris asked Packer Fullback Nick Luchey on the Larry McCarren Locker Room Show.

"I sure do," Nick said. "My mom prays with me every week before the game."

"Good question, Chris." Larry patted the young man's shoulder before he returned to his seat, and *then* I breathed. Chris was born with Down Syndrome, and as his mother, I find myself holding my breath a lot. Chris often amazes me with what he says. There are also times when we have long talks about what not to say the next time.

We enjoy occasionally attending Larry's show on Monday nights. Larry "The Rock" McCarren was center for the Packers from 1973-1984 and is a member of the Packer Hall of Fame.[22] His show is broadcast to all of northeast Wisconsin and much of Michigan's Upper Peninsula.

It is a live TV show, so I was a little concerned when Chris insisted on asking a question. I tried to stall him, to no avail, and somehow he managed to get near the front of the line.

I don't know what would have happened if the guest did not have faith, but somehow I know he would have recognized the faith of many Packer players and fans. As it was, he gave Chris a great answer and me a great sigh of relief.

Chris is as big a Packer fan as me, and he actually keeps better track of the schedule than do I. I wear my Packer clothes often. Chris wears his almost every day.

Faith in God can be part and parcel of our lives, or it can be something a bit nebulous or far-fetched. For Chris, it's a part of everyday life. It wasn't just a cute question, one that he really didn't understand. No, it was a very real concern because, as a Packer fan, Chris wants the players to have that same faith: one, so they'll go to heaven; and two, so they'll play their best.

Can you ask Chris' question? Can you answer it with ease?

EXTRA POINT:

Lord, help me to always be ready to speak an answer about my faith in You.

Who's Watching You?

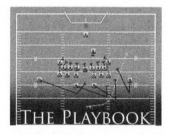

FROM THE PLAYBOOK:

"Therefore we also, since we are surrounded by so great a cloud of witnesses, let us lay aside every weight, and the sin which so easily ensnares us, and let us run with endurance the race that is set before us."

Hebrews 12:1

Who can forget the Monday night playoff game at the Oakland Raiders' in December of 2003? Brett Favre's dad had just died. Brett had a cloud of fans in the stands back in Wisconsin and around the world that cheered him on, wished him well, and prayed for his strength and comfort. He knew it. He felt it. And he appreciated it.

At the time, he felt his dad watching him, his wife and family loving him, and his teammates supporting him. Every one of them, along with the fans, would have understood if he chose not to play that night. No one would have faulted him, except perhaps his dad, forever the coach. His dad instilled the love of the game in Brett as well as the passion to always play to win.[23]

The Bible says we are surrounded by a great cloud of witnesses—those who have gone to heaven before us. These witnesses want us to make it. They want us to press on, and they want us to know that the One within us is greater than anything or any loss we experience in this life.

Like a stadium of fans, they cheer us on, rejoice with our success, and encourage us to hang in there when it's tough. Brett experienced the power of witnesses in Oakland that night, but God wants us to experience it every single day of our lives.

What are you facing? Do you know it's never just your will, your faith, or your determination that gets you through?

Brett Favre wanted to win for Green Bay. He wanted to continue his amazing record of consecutive starts. He wanted to make his dad proud, but that wasn't what carried him. It was the great cloud of fans who cheered and prayed for him, along with his teammates and family members who supported him. It was the words of his dad that he heard all his life that spoke within him.

We are not alone. We have fans. We have God, and we have His voice and His Word within us. Press on today and watch the wondrous miracles that can take place.

EXTRA POINT:

Lord, I will press through difficult times so I can run the race You set before me, knowing You and all Your people are cheering me on.

Behind the Scenes

1 Peter 2:9-25

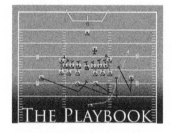

THE PLAYBOOK

FROM THE PLAYBOOK:

But you are a chosen generation, a royal priesthood . . . that you may proclaim the praises of Him who called you out of darkness into His marvelous light.

1 Peter 2:9

"To Cheri the angel. Save me a spot. Aaron Rodgers." So read the autographed football given to the father of a young girl who had passed away. Aaron was a guest at a charity event for an organization that supported eliminating childhood cancer and blood disorders. It was not televised or highly publicized, but Aaron shared his heart and his time.[24]

The event occurred before the beginning of the 2010 season, which would see Aaron become the Super Bowl Most Valuable Player. What an honor! And well deserved. He threw for 300 yards, had one running touchdown, and never got intercepted. His whole season was stellar. Perhaps the heart and ethic of this man is as much revealed in small gatherings as it is in big games.

When asked at the charity event what his favorite book was, Aaron didn't hesitate in saying the Bible and that he tries to read it every day. What's exciting to know is that because of

Aaron's faith, he most certainly will get to see little Cheri upon his arrival in heaven one day.

Aaron Rodgers is not as outgoing in sharing his faith as perhaps Greg Jennings or Reggie White. However, his relationship with the Lord is real and evident in his upstanding character. And, most importantly, he is not shy about it. When asked, he openly shares.

Isn't it refreshing to see young men, athletically strong, successful, and financially well-off, professing Christ as Savior? Isn't it sad that sometimes we are surprised that someone who seems to have it all in the natural is also strong spiritually? It really should be the norm.

Where do you stand? Does spiritual strength seem incongruous with natural strength?

Imagine if all of us fulfilled all that God has placed in us both naturally and spiritually. What would this world look like? Perhaps the quality of life would be several levels higher than it is. The best way to find out is to decide that your life, from this point on, will be top caliber in every area.

EXTRA POINT:

Lord, I stand before You now, and I pledge to ratchet my attention up to quality living with Your help and for Your glory.

Feet Feat

Hebrews 12:7-15

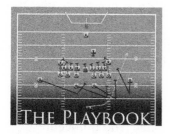

FROM THE PLAYBOOK:

Make straight paths for your feet, so that what is lame may not be dislocated, but rather be healed.

Hebrews 12:13

Both feet down. Impossible or so it seemed. Jordy Nelson, a Packers wide receiver. One of the fastest players, if not the fastest, in the NFL.

The pass, just in front of his route, on second and ten, designed so the cornerback couldn't get it. The Giants trailed one point behind the Packers, 28-27, at home on December 4, 2011. With just under four minutes left in the game, Jordy rose up, grasped that ball, spun around, and brought both feet down in bounds for a 21-yard gain. Of course it was challenged, but the Giants lost the challenge. And they lost the game, by a Mason Crosby 30-yard field goal in the final seconds, 38-35.

Jordy's response to the fantastic feat of his feet was, "You didn't know I was a ballet dancer. I'd like to think I'm a pretty good athlete."[25] Two plays later, Donald Driver caught a 7-yard bullet from Rodgers, tapping his toes in the corner of the end zone to put the Packers up 35-27. Perhaps it was that play that made Driver decide to be part of the show *Dancing With the Stars* after the 2011 season ended.

We don't know if Jordy is considering doing that, but an athlete he is. In just the 2011 season, he had sixty-eight receptions for 1263 yards and fifteen touchdowns.

Where are your feet? Are they on the right path, in the right route? When you go up for a catch, are they disciplined enough to come down in bounds? Do you know if you are fit to play the role you're in? It takes training and coordination. Do most of us ever think about where our feet are? How about spiritually? Do your feet go where they are supposed to?

There are a lot of spiritual paths to go down. Can you choose the right ones or do you go wherever it seems fun or pleasant or lucrative? We've heard stories of people who innocently—or so it seemed—started down a path that ended up costing them years of their lives along with great pain and disappointment.

Most people don't end up on a successful path by happenstance. They have to choose to work hard, prepare, and train daily. That's what football players do with their feet, as do dancers. Our lives are a whole package. Every part affects the other parts. Let's notice where our feet take us and where we take our feet. Let's be the one who comes down in bounds and grabs a win for our team.

Extra Point:

Lord, help me keep my feet in bounds and on track every day.

Great Promises

2 Peter 1:2-12

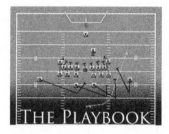

FROM THE PLAYBOOK:

By which have been given to us exceeding great and precious promises that through these you may be partakers of the divine nature.

2 Peter 1:4

Do you own a piece of the Pack? I do, as over 112,000 people have for many years. That number rose to 350,000 at the end of 2011. It is the only franchise in the National Football League that is owned by the fans.[26] Being a shareholder is an honor. Perhaps because so many of us own the Packers, we say "we" when we talk about the team and the games.

President Obama now owns a piece of the Pack. Charles Woodson presented one share to him when he welcomed the Green Bay Packer World Champions to the White House in August of 2011.

The President had planned to go to the Super Bowl only if Chicago beat the Packers in the NFC Championship Game. Woodson previously chided the President about not attending and proclaimed the Packers would visit him at the White House. The President admitted it was hard to congratulate the Packers, but he did. He also hoped his share in the Pack would give him some decision-making power. Woodson let him know, with a chuckle, that it did not.[27]

We are all shareholders in God's blessings. We have been given great and precious promises that allow us to take part in the life and love of God. Whether we exercise our rights or choose to dismiss them is up to us.

When the Packers have their annual shareholder's meeting each July, I am invited to attend, but I must vote for the board members in order to get my free ticket. It is my choice. When I attended in July of 2011, I had my picture taken with Packer President Mark Murphy, looked up-close at the Packer Super Bowl Ring, and toured the Hall of Fame for free. The years I don't go, I don't enjoy special privileges.

When I read the Bible and see great privileges awarded to those who believe, I decide to engage and participate or I ignore the opportunity and go my way.

The problem is, when I don't participate, I find myself wondering why life is such a struggle. Believing and standing strong on promises for peace, healing, direction, and wisdom can also be a struggle, but the results are so much better than struggling to survive.

We can be fans of God, but how much better it is to be a shareholder in all the blessings Jesus died to give us.

EXTRA POINT:

Lord, I choose to learn my rights and privileges as a shareholder in Your inheritance and participate in every one.

The Harvest is Ready

Ecclesiastes 9:10-18

FROM THE PLAYBOOK:

Whatever your hand finds to do, do it with your might.

Ecclesiastes 9:10

What does faith have to do with football? It's a question many ask. Football is a platform for many players to share their faith. It is also an avenue for them to follow their gifting well, bringing honor to God.

In the classic movie, *Chariots of Fire*, we watch the true story of Eric Liddell, a young man from Scotland. His character states, "I feel God's pleasure when I run."[28] His testimony became national news when he chose not to run on a Sunday during the 1924 Olympics, honoring the Sabbath. Some would suggest that proves football players dishonor God by playing sixteen Sundays of the year.

But I ask does God feel pleasure at a great sack, a strong block, a pass like a bullet, and a Lambeau Leap after a touchdown? I suspect many players, like Eric Liddell, feel God's pleasure when they play well.

The Bible calls God the Lord of the Harvest. He looks at his fields, ready to be harvested, and He sends workers out to the right place at the right time to bring in the results of all His labor. In the Bible, the harvest is the analogy of people coming into God's kingdom or being born again. God's purpose as the Lord of the harvest is to bring people into relationship with Him.

Can football do that? Can being a real estate salesman do that? How about a teacher, a repairman, a doctor, or a store owner? The harvest is everywhere, in every walk of life. So, God equips and sends people into every area and strata of society. Football is a place where players can help bring in the harvest of other football players and influence thousands of fans.

What is your sphere of influence? Are you able to be a worker in the harvest of the Lord? Most of us have many areas where we can let our light shine. Let's pray for every worker to be effective in the harvest, no matter where it may be. See if maybe you feel God's pleasure when the Packers make a Lambeau Leap.

EXTRA POINT:

Whatever I find to do, Lord, help me to do it with all my might and bring You glory.

Samson's Cousin?

Philippians 4:4-20

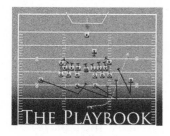

THE PLAYBOOK

FROM THE PLAYBOOK:

I can do all things through Christ who strengthens me.

Philippians 4:13

"**H**air on Fire." That's Clay Matthews III, grandson of Clay Sr., son of Clay Jr., and nephew of Bruce. Together, these linebackers have a combined forty-two years of NFL experience. Clay's grandfather spent four years on the offensive line with the San Francisco Forty-Niners. His dad played nineteen years as a linebacker for the Browns and the Falcons, playing his last playoff game against the Packers at Lambeau on December 31, 1995. Uncle Bruce spent nineteen years playing linebacker for the Houston Oilers and the Tennessee Titans.[29]

Obviously, Matthews grew up in football, and although his parents never pushed, Clay found the fire was in his heart. Have you seen him blaze through a team's offensive line? Have you seen him wrap up a quarterback? Have you seen his long blond hair?

Between the third and fourth quarters of the Super Bowl, Outside Linebackers Coach Kevin Greene looked at Matthews and said, "It's time."[30] They both knew the rest of that sentence would be "to make a game change." As runner-up NFL Defensive Player of the Year, Matthews knew what had to be done.

Rashad Mendenhall of the Pittsburgh Steelers had the ball on the next play. The play was meant to go the left but it was adjusted to the right. Matthews hit Mendenhall hard on the elbow. Out came the ball, and it was picked up by Linebacker Desmond Bishop. That play set up a Packer touchdown, propelling them to their 31-25 win and the first Super Bowl ring for the Matthews family.

Matthews' enthusiasm is catching. Intensity, training, and persistence are three characteristics that you see in this young man. What follows those traits? Results!

It's easy to hold back for all sorts of reasons that sound good. Respect. Balance. Safety. Those reasons have their place, but where has God put you? What is necessary to complete God's purpose for you in your calling? Can you be the "Hair on Fire" that ignites those around you to do their best?

Sometimes we need to step back and take another look at who we are and who we are destined to be. Are those two things one and the same? Can you make the changes necessary? With God's help and with time in the Bible, you will be able to do everything God designed you to do.

EXTRA POINT:

Lord, help me be all that You designed me to be.

Can You Do Quantum Physics?

2 Timothy 3:10-17

THE PLAYBOOK

FROM THE PLAYBOOK:

All scripture is given by inspiration of God, and is profitable for doctrine, for reproof, for correction, for instruction in righteousness.

2 Timothy 3:16

"It's like learning quantum physics in Chinese," commented a Packer 2011 draft pick about the playbook.[31] The NFL lockout gave rookies precious little time to prepare for the season.

Getting drafted has to be a thrill. Then you have to perform, prove yourself all over again, compete for position, and give everything you've got while avoiding injury. It's a tall order, but rookies embrace it eagerly.

The best part of that process is the team. Veteran players and coaches are there to assist, instruct, encourage, and toughen you up. There's competition for position, as well as camaraderie. It may seem like quantum physics in Chinese at first, but amazingly, it becomes second nature for those who focus, practice, and stay disciplined.

Many have the same sense when beginning to read the

Bible. As the playbook is the key to playing the game well, the Bible is the key to living life well. It's important to remember we're part of a team. We have fellow believers to assist, instruct, encourage, and yes, even toughen us up. We have the added bonus of the Father, Son, and Holy Spirit living inside us to guide our steps in the paths of life.

A football player, veteran or rookie, who keeps practicing, while staying focused and disciplined, will undoubtedly be a good player. Most likely, they'll become a great player.

Are you willing to delve into the Bible and learn? Are you willing to practice obeying the Bible, even when it seems you're on a losing team? Keep at it and soon you'll have a lifestyle that honors God and blesses those around you.

EXTRA POINT:

Lord, I'm willing to learn, even though I feel like a rookie in some areas. Help me to keep at it.

Where is Your Trust?

Psalm 20:1 – Psalm 21:3

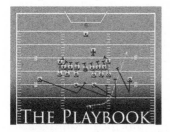

FROM THE PLAYBOOK:

Some trust in chariots, and some in horses; but we will remember the name of the Lord our God.

Psalm 20:7

Playing a January game against a southern team in outdoor Lambeau Field is a delicious thought for Packer Fans. We wanted to make the Atlanta Falcons come to the Frozen Tundra for the 2010 playoffs. It wasn't to be. Games lost by three or four points almost knocked us out of the playoffs altogether. We held on. Atlanta was the first seed. The Packers were sixth seed, the wildcard.

Now the tables were turned. We would go to Atlanta, where the Falcons rarely lost. This Falcon team seemed a formidable obstacle. Besides being dominating, they had a week off right before the game to rest and heal, and they had already beaten us earlier in the season.

Amazingly, the Packers commanded a 21-14 lead late in the first half. Atlanta drove down the field looking to tie the game. The Packer defense held, and it looked as though Atlanta would settle for a field goal. However, the man with the lion's mane, Clay Matthews, got a sack on Quarterback Matt Ryan. It pushed Atlanta out of field goal range, but they had time for one more play. Ryan passed, intending to get the Falcons back in field goal range. Instead, Tramon Williams intercepted and ran seventy yards for a touchdown. Packer fans went wild. Halftime score was 28-14.[32]

Rodgers maintained the momentum, gaining two more touchdowns in the third quarter. The Packer defense stuffed and stopped a baffled Atlanta offense. The final score of 48-21 left the Falcons surprised and befuddled. They felt their crushing loss.

Most of the football world was shocked with them, but not the Packers. All season long they remained true to their commitment. They would not give up and they would get to the Super Bowl. They did not get cocky or arrogant about their ability, but they remained confident. They trusted each other, and they played for the team, not just themselves.

Where is your confidence? Is your confidence actually arrogance, or is it that calm assurance that keeps pulling you forward despite the obstacles? In 1 John 5:14-15 we are told, "Now this is the confidence that we have in Him, that if we ask anything according to His will, He hears us. And if we know that He hears us, whatever we ask, we know that we have the petitions that we have asked of Him."

Our assurance is born in faith that God's Word, the Bible, is true. In the Bible and in prayer, we find God's will for our lives. Then we have the confidence to live it out, work at it, work with it, and keep working even when the odds are against us. When we persevere through the difficulties, we begin to see the fulfillment of God's will for us.

Don't let the first seed intimidate you when you're a sixth seed, a wildcard in the eyes of the world. Play your game and keep doing what you know is right. You may surprise yourself.

EXTRA POINT:

Lord, help me to remain true to You, no matter what.

The Requirement

Micah 6:6-8

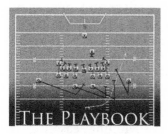

FROM THE PLAYBOOK:

He has shown you, O man, what is good; And what does the Lord require of you But to do justly, To love mercy, And to walk humbly with your God?

Micah 6:8

"**N**o penalties and not turning the ball over, that's a good formula for winning."[33] Coach McCarthy spoke of the Christmas Day 2011 game against the Chicago Bears. The Packers had their first penalty free game since November 15, 1990.

Two seasons earlier, the Packers led the penalty count for the entire NFL with 118. On September 27, 2010, the Packers lost to the Bears 20-17 with a franchise high of eighteen penalties in one game.

McCarthy's directive following that game was short and to the point: "Enough is enough!"[34] By November 21, 2010, the Packers had a one penalty game. Frank Zombo had been called for five yards due to a neutral zone infraction. From then on, the highest number of penalties in any regular or post-season game was seven.

An area where penalties easily occur is in cornerback coverage. Charles Woodson, outstanding in his cornerback position, was penalized twelve times in the 2010 season, the team high. In the 2011 season, that number dropped to six. Cornerback Tramon Williams had no penalties in the 2011 season, and Nickel Cornerback Sam Shields also had zero.

Joe Whitt, cornerbacks coach, said, "If we can get our feet into position first and then bring our hands in and understand our bump levels, hopefully we won't get called for penalties."[35]

No doubt, penalty-free playing was emphasized at every meeting and every practice. Focus, determination, and discipline are necessary for every player. Without an individual and team effort, penalties would escalate. The more penalties, the less likely a team will have a win or a winning season.

How fitting the Packers brought all that effort and discipline together to play penalty-free on Christmas Day. And against da Bears!

We all make mistakes, and we have an amazingly forgiving God. But, like the cornerbacks, we need to take the time to get our feet and our hands into position so that fewer mistakes occur in the first place. How do we do that?

It takes time to sit down with the Lord and present our day, our goals, our obstacles and concerns to Him. We need to see what guidance the Bible provides for the many situations of daily life: right choices, refusing anger, being diligent, loving mercy, doing justly, and walking humbly with God. We need to listen to His coaching voice within ourselves and follow His leading.

As we do that, we'll see fewer and fewer penalties in our days and more and more winning seasons in our lives.

EXTRA POINT:

Thank You, Father, that I can walk with You daily and that You have shown me what is good. I commit to loving mercy, doing justly, and walking humbly with You.

Have Fun. Now Get Back to Work.

Romans 12:1-5

FROM THE PLAYBOOK:

For I say, through the grace given to me, to everyone who is among you, not to think of himself more highly than he ought to think.

Romans 12:3

Cameras, smiles, laughter. Media Day before the Big Game. Stories, jokes, mild exhaustion, media hysteria. Packer players were asked serious and silly questions, and they loved every minute of it. Playing in the Super Bowl made them stars. Many players took their own photos and videos of themselves to remember the experience.

They knew they deserved to be there. They had won the right with hard work and perseverance. However, they chose to enjoy Media Day while not getting caught in the hype of thinking of themselves as superstars. They enjoyed the day and then refocused on their purpose to not just play in the Super Bowl, but to win it.

Fame can be wonderful, but it has been the avenue to great downfalls. Talent and hard work should be rewarded, but maintaining a humble spirit can be a real challenge.

Even Jesus faced that challenge when he met up with Satan in the wilderness. He was seeking God's direction with all His heart. Satan took Him up on the pinnacle of Jerusalem and offered Him all the kingdoms of the world. All Jesus had to do was bow down and submit to Satan and his ways. Thankfully for all of us, Jesus told him to get lost. Let's face it, Jesus is the ruler of all, and He did things God's way.

The Packers could have been intimidated by the media scrutiny and adulation. They could have been sucked into grandiose beliefs about themselves, but instead, they took a day off to enjoy themselves and the media, and then they went back to work. Team work, good coaches, good friends, and perhaps the small town feel of Green Bay, contributed to their balanced approach.

Are you careful not to think more highly of yourself than you ought to? There's nothing wrong with enjoying the fruits of your hard work, talent, and perseverance, but be sure to maintain humility and thankfulness in the midst of it. Letting others put you on a pedestal puts you in place where it's easy to take a big fall. Let's keep our eyes on God, enjoy His blessings, and focus on the next steps in our lives rather than the adulations.

EXTRA POINT:

I will keep my eyes on You, Lord, not on me, so that I may see the next step.

Teamwork is Monumental

1 Corinthians 1:1-10

FROM THE PLAYBOOK:

Now I plead with you, brethren, by the name of our Lord Jesus Christ, that you all speak the same thing, and that there be no divisions among you, but that you be perfectly joined together in the same mind and in the same judgment.

1 Corinthians 1:10

Do you ever consider the trust level of the wide receiver as he goes all out to catch a pass? Any number of defensive players will pound him into the ground to get him to let go of that ball or at least gain no additional yards after the catch. Head injuries, shoulder injuries, season-ending injuries have occurred, yet play after play those receivers want nothing more than the chance to catch the pass for their team.

Donald Driver will smile and say it's just part of the game. He and other receivers seem to delight in popping up after what appears to be a devastating blow. What we don't see is the daily fitness regime they put themselves through in order to withstand those blows. Equally important is the trust they have in each other.

They may not always say it but they know their teammates and trust them to block and throw the defense off their attack. Reporters often comment on the camaraderie in the locker room as a basis for that trust. Players comment on it as well. The atmosphere in the locker room sets the tone for the game. When NFL teams don't play well, you often hear that the locker room had a lot of tension. The Packers have been known for their positive locker room and good teamwork.

Who has your back? Where is your trust in your daily life? Is it in friends, family, church, or coworkers? Is God on your side? The Bible teaches us that if we belong to Him, then He is for us. If you fellowship with others who know God is for them, then you will have a team of believers to support you, pray for you, encourage you, and pull together with you in any situation.

Who can trust you? Are you a team player with friends, church members, and coworkers? Do others know they can depend on you to have their back? The Bible tells us not to let there be divisions among us but to love and support one another. A tall order? Perhaps. But, as we obey the Biblical instruction to love others, we will prove ourselves trustworthy, a teammate that others will want to associate with and support.

EXTRA POINT:

Lord, help me become a trustworthy teammate to those who are in my life.

Privileges of Ownership

1 Corinthians 2:6-16

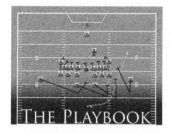

FROM THE PLAYBOOK:

Now we have received . . . the Spirit who is from God, that we might know the things that have been freely given to us by God.

1 Corinthians 2:12

On shareholder day at Lambeau Field, I was leaving the Packer Hall of Fame with my son. He wanted to take the elevator rather than the stairs. As the doors opened, two men with their backs to me stepped off the elevator in the opposite direction. As the doors were closing, I realized they were Jordy Nelson and Greg Jennings, wide receivers for the Packers.

I wanted to call out their names and talk to them, but the doors closed. A man who got on from that hallway told me the hall went to the locker room, and no, I couldn't go down there.

Due to position and employment, certain people have access to places and other people. Even though I'm a Packer shareholder, I do not have access to the locker room.

It's the same where you work and where you live. You have privileges not available to those who don't live or work there. People without connections have restrictions.

It's also the same with God. If we know Him, we have access to Him and to His blessings. If God is in you, He has given you access to Himself and all that He is. The Bible says that we "live and move and have our being" in Him (Acts 17:28). That is total access.

It would be silly if Greg Jennings asked the coach if he could get into the locker room after the game. Yet, many of us think we're imposing on God when we ask Him for personal blessings and to meet our needs. He has opened the door of access wide for us, and we need to choose to "know the things freely given us by God."

How do we do that? First, we receive Jesus as our Lord and Savior. Next, we begin reading the Bible and find a church we can belong to. Most importantly, we learn that God is in us, for us, and with us and that His Word, the Bible, is true. The more we believe the Bible, the more we'll realize we have access to His promises. It is quite an amazing journey. We won't be wishing we could run down the hall to get God's attention. He'll be with us in every step and in every moment of our lives.

EXTRA POINT:

Lord, I choose You, and I choose to believe Your Word. Thank you that more and more I will know all the things you have provided for me.

Shoulda, Woulda, Coulda

Hebrews 4:9-16

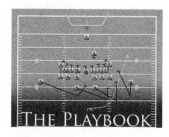

FROM THE PLAYBOOK:

Let us therefore come boldly to the throne of grace, that we may obtain mercy and find grace to help in time of need.

Heb. 4:16

It was painful. I had to take a lesson from Tim Tebow.

The Packers lost to the Giants. Again. In Lambeau. In January. When the Super Bowl was on the line.

Were the Packers rusty? They'd rested top players the final game of the regular season, then had a one week bye, so three weeks without play had passed. Team members felt rested and ready.

Offensive Coach Joe Philbin's son had died tragically in a drowning accident the week before the game. When something like that happens, big games slide down the list of importance. It was tough for the team.[36] People don't always realize how profoundly grief affects their thinking skills and their ability to focus.

The sixth-seed Giants ran rough shod over the first seed Packers, just as the sixth-seed Packers had done to the first-seed Falcons the year before. There were fumbles, drops, and terrible plays, and the final score was 37-20.[37]

How does Tim Tebow play into all of this? The media frenzy over his faith, his comebacks, and his bowing to pray, or "Tebowing," was at its height. Behind the scenes, Tim brought needy people to the game and spent time with them before and after. Following a big Denver loss, a young woman, wheelchair bound, told how Tim came in and said, "Well, that certainly didn't go as planned." He then conversed with her as if nothing else mattered but her.[38] That's impressive.

After our big loss, my son reminded me that the coach in the movie *Facing the Giants* (appropriate title that day) had recited with his team, "If we win, we'll praise the Lord, and if we lose, we'll praise the Lord."

It seemed a sure thing that the Packers would bring home another Lombardi trophy, and that wasn't going to happen now. I could mourn and complain, or I could follow two great examples and say, "That sure wasn't what we planned, and though I'm disappointed, I will praise the Lord and pray for the team, especially Coach Philbin." In the light of eternity, the game loss was a small thing. But when effort and dreams are thwarted, it can be very big and tough. If we keep our eyes on the Lord, He will help us look past the difficulties, to the bright future He has for all of us and help us focus on the most important things, which usually aren't things.

EXTRA POINT:
Thank You, Lord, that You keep my perspective right.

Can You Leap?

Acts 3:1-16

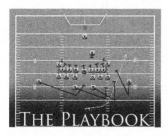

FROM THE PLAYBOOK:

So he, leaping up, stood and walked and entered the temple with them – walking, leaping, and praising God.

Acts 3:8

"As long as they throw him back, I think it's great."[39] Those were Coach Holmgren's words when asked what he thought about the Lambeau Leap.

The first Lambeau Leap was by Packer Safety Leroy Butler in 1993. The Packers played the Oakland Raiders. Reggie picked up a fumble and tossed it laterally to Butler, who took it to the end zone for six points. Butler ran to the stands and jumped. Some described him as looking like a magnet – he stuck to the wall as the fans grabbed him.

In 1995, Robert Brooks, wide receiver, decided to improve on Butler's jump. He planned to jump into the stands, not just hang on. It was an instant success and became the signature touchdown celebration for the Packers.

"It just doesn't get any better than jumping into the arms of those fans," said Brooks. "It's just a natural reaction now after a touchdown. I start dashing through the end zone to spend time with the greatest fans in the world who pay our salaries and love us so much."[40]

Celebration is a wonderful thing. When we become Christians, we aren't expected to check our emotions at the door. Instead, we get our emotions anointed. They become balanced and honest. Joy is the best. The Bible tells us, "The joy of the Lord is our strength (Nehemiah 8:10)." It doesn't mean we go around with silly grins and ridiculous antics; we have a deep reservoir of smiling peace. We know our God is for us and will see us through any difficulty we have. When things are going well, it's OK to dance, and when things are not going well, it's OK to trust with joyful expectation that God will turn things around.

Can you celebrate today? Can you be thankful for at least one thing? Can you rejoice that God is truly on your side? Do you know that if you get that touchdown, it's all right to leap into the stands?

Extra Point:

Lord, thank You for celebrating triumphs with me and giving me the freedom to rejoice.

Be Quick To Pray

Proverbs 15:21-24

FROM THE PLAYBOOK:

A man has joy by the answer of his mouth.

Proverbs 15:23

Brett Favre suffered a severe ankle sprain in the middle of the 1995 season. It occurred during a game against the Vikings in the Minneapolis Metrodome. The Packers lost the game, and Brett could hardly walk the next day.

However, it was the season of miraculous healings a la Reggie White. Brett recounted, "Hey, I'm not as spiritual a person as Reggie, but the big man asked if he could put some oil on my forehead and pray for me. I said, 'Sure.'"[41]

The following week, the Bears visited Lambeau, hoping to capitalize on an injured Favre. Brett had a great game, and the Packers won 35-28. Brett also won the Most Valuable Player award at the end of the season.

What if Brett had said no to Reggie? The season might have been very different. His ankle would have healed, but would it have happened so quickly? Isn't that what a miracle is, the speeding up of the natural process, unexplained by natural causes?

What if Reggie hadn't asked? How many times do we

hesitate to ask, because we are quite sure that the person doesn't believe as we do?

How many people secretly hope we'll pray, even though they do not ask? How many opportunities are lost because we hesitate to ask someone if we can pray for them? Perhaps their need is great. Sometimes it's small. But, the need is there, and it is an invitation for us to share the love and power of our God.

Let's be quick to pray, and perhaps, like Brett and Reggie, we'll see outstanding results.

EXTRA POINT:

Lord, help me to be quick to pray, always expecting the best.

Give Honor to Whom It is Due

Psalm 126:1-6

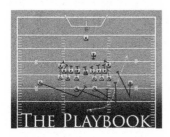

FROM THE PLAYBOOK:

Then our mouth was filled with laughter, And our tongue with singing. Then they said among the nations, "The Lord has done great things for them."

Psalm 126:2

We stood on our feet and cheered for Yancey Thigpen, wide receiver for the Pittsburg Steelers, with every Packer fan in Lambeau Field. How could that be? It was preseason 1996, and the sportscasters announced the opposing players, who ran onto the field. It was spontaneous and totally heartfelt. We knew why we stood and cheered for this Pro Bowl receiver on the other team.

It began on Christmas Eve 1995. The last twenty seconds of the regular season. Fourth down on the 16-yard line. Pittsburgh quarterback, Neil O'Donnell, threw the winning pass to Yancey Thigpen, who waited in the end zone.

I was in Detroit for Christmas, watching with family members who rooted for Tampa Bay, Dallas, and the Lions. I ignored their teasing that we would lose home field advantage in the playoffs due to this loss. I prayed. A Packer win and the

Division Title would be a great Christmas gift from the Lord.

But there was Thigpen in the end zone and the pass came right to him. There would be no time for us get another score. Still, I prayed and held my breath.

And then it happened. How could it happen? Yancey Thigpen dropped the ball in the end zone! The winning pass slipped through his fingers, hit his knee, and landed on the ground. The Packers won. We won the game! We won the Central Division title for the first time in twenty-three years.[42]

We were very thankful to Yancey Thigpen that first game of the preseason. He knew why we gave him a standing ovation and laughed about it. What else could he do? His drop sent us soaring. He deserved our accolade.

A Pro-Bowl receiver in the end zone dropping an easy pass? Unbelievable—unless you are a believer.

How many unbelievable things have happened in your life? Not everyone would call Thigpen's dropped ball a miracle. It's all in the perspective. We believe, we pray, we expect, and when our prayers are answered, we know it's God. Others see a coincidence, a happenstance, luck, even a mistake. You see answers to prayer, blessings, and miracles.

Life is better from God's perspective. But, it's not always a comfortable way to live. Sometimes the miracle we need takes great trust in the God we love. As we make daily choices to walk in faith, to believe the Bible, to know the God who made us and His Son who died for us, we'll find our eyes see beyond the natural to the supernatural power of a loving God.

EXTRA POINT:

Lord, as I endeavor to make my perspective Your perspective, open my eyes to see beyond the natural.

Chemistry

Ecclesiastes 4

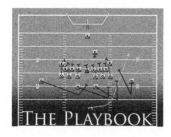

THE PLAYBOOK

FROM THE PLAYBOOK:

Two are better than one, because they have a good (more satisfying) reward for their labor; For if they fall, the one will lift up his fellow. But woe to him who is alone when he falls and has not another to lift him up!

Ecclesiastes 4: 9, 10 (AB)

13 and 0. December 11, 2011. It had never happened in Packer history. How sweet was Ryan Grant's run? In a season of many records, 2011 had not seen a long touchdown run. Grant's longest run had been fourteen yards. With 11:57 left in the first quarter against the Oakland Raiders, Center Scott Wells and Left Guard TJ Lang opened up the Oakland defense. As a result, Oakland Linebacker Rolando McClain got a bad angle, and Grant, with his great footwork, dodged through and sprinted forty-seven yards for a touchdown.[43]

Rookie Linebacker DJ Smith had set up the early touchdown by intercepting the Oakland ball when Quarterback Palmer underthrew his receiver on their first drive. The game held four more take-aways, and the game ended in a 46-16 Packer win. It placed the Packers winning streak at nineteen. Almost a whole year had passed without a loss.[44]

With all those great plays and records set, Aaron Rodgers had his lowest rating of the season, 96.7. Many thought if Aaron's play was off, the game was lost. That's a big factor, but not the only one. The rest of the team stepped up with great blocks, interceptions, and good catches.

Chemistry is an interesting thing. The goal is for everyone to play at the top of their game, but the reality is that it does not always happen. If everyone strives for that, then the occasional lower level play of one or two team members is covered by the rest.

Ever have an off day? Did you have a teammate who could cover for you? Are you ready and willing to cover for your friends and family? Team chemistry is much like Bible brotherhood. We're not just looking for our own success. We're also looking for the success of the body of Christ, our fellow believers. Instead of pointing the finger when someone fails or falls, we simply step up our game to fill in the gaps. The Bible calls it love, and in 1 Peter 4:8 we are told that "love covers a multitude of sins."

A win is a win whether it's a blow-out 46-14 against the Raiders or a squeaker win by a field goal in the final seconds against the Giants. Let's be suited up and ready to help our teammates.

EXTRA POINT:

Thank You, Lord, that You and Your children have my back. Help me be ready to step in when my teammates need me.

Sweet Results

Hebrews 3:1-14

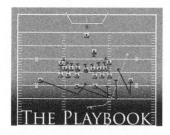

THE PLAYBOOK

FROM THE PLAYBOOK:

For we have become partakers of Christ if we hold the beginning of our confidence steadfast to the end.

Hebrews 3:14

"**N**othing better than that right now." Brian Urlacher, Chicago Bears linebacker, referred to knocking the Packers out of the 2010 season playoffs. The comment came five days before the last game of the season. The Bears were the division champs and already in the playoffs. A win against the Packers would not improve their seed.[45]

In that position, most teams rest their first string players so they're fresh and injury-free for the playoffs. Not the Bears. A Packer win would make Green Bay a wild card in the playoffs, and Chicago wanted the Packers out.

The game was the first time in the history of the Packers/ Bears series that Chicago visited Green Bay in the season finale. It was January 2, 2010 and would be the last game of the season or the first game of the playoffs for the Packers. The Bears had beaten them in Chicago by three points earlier in the season. The Packers had too many penalties during that game and turned the ball over twice—a sure recipe for loss.

Many Packer fans thought that last game of the season would be an easy win, as it seemed certain Chicago would not play their starters. Instead, the starters played the whole game, hoping to keep the Packers far away from the road to the Super Bowl.

It was a defensive game, 3-0 at halftime, with a Bears field goal being the only score. The second half began with joy for the Bears. Aaron Rodgers was intercepted on the first play. Late in the third quarter, Rodgers connected with Jennings on a 33-yard pass, giving the Packers a first down on the 1-yard line. The Bears defense held and the Packers scored only a field goal.

On the Packers' next drive, they got to the 1-yard line again, the result of another big pass to Jennings. The following play was a touchdown pass to Donald Lee, and the Packers were ahead 10-3.

Less than a minute remained in the game. Chicago made it to the Packers' 32-yard line. Bears quarterback, Jay Cutler, fired a pass, sure to set-up a Chicago win. It went right into the hands of Packer Safety Nick Collins. The Packers made it to the play-offs.[46]

I'm sure there was a collective groan across Bear land. The Bears knew the Packers were hot and capable. Chicago knew they may well meet us again in the playoffs.

Life is full of "what ifs" and "if onlys." The Bears thought they covered it by playing their starters, sure they could bump us off. The Packers knew their post-season began with that game. Any loss would bump them out. Playing with persistence and heart was necessary for the Packers.

It is so important for us as well. The thing we desire can only be achieved if we persist with all our heart. Sometimes it's tough. Sometimes it hurts. But, the end result is so sweet. Hang in there. It may seem that the Bears' starters are doing all they can to knock you out of the game, but God will help you keep going. With God's help, you'll be on the field for the next game and the next.

EXTRA POINT:

Lord, I thank You for strength and confidence to hang in there and do all You have called me to do.

Renew Your Youth

Psalm 103:1-5

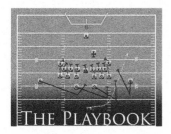

FROM THE PLAYBOOK:

Who satisfies your mouth with good things, So that your youth is renewed like the eagle's.

Psalm 103:5

"He looks like he's twenty-two," said Cornerback Coach Joe Whitt of Charles Woodson. Charles Woodson, actually in his mid-thirties, arrived at the 2011 training camp in the best shape of his career.[47] This was after breaking his collarbone late in the second quarter of the Super Bowl.

The thirteen-year veteran dove in hopes of getting a Super Bowl interception and fell hard on his left side. "I knew it was broken," he said later. Undoubtedly out of the game, Woodson tried to encourage the team at halftime. He broke down as he tried to tell them what the game meant to him. Finally he told them, "Just win!"

Woodson played in the Super Bowl after the 2002 season. He was with the Oakland Raiders and lost to Tampa Bay. He had many awards—the 1997 Heisman Trophy while at University of Michigan, NFL Defensive Rookie of the Year, NFL Defensive Player of the Year, and several Pro Bowls—but never a Super Bowl win.[48] That broken collar bone almost broke his heart.

After the NFC Championship win against the Chicago

Bears, the Packers united under Woodson's request to play with "one mind, one goal, one purpose, and one heart." It pumped up the team and drove their determination to win so much that they agreed the phrase should be inscribed on the Packer Super Bowl Rings.[49] It would also come to grace the famous fence that stands facing Lambeau Field, which has a great phrase painted on it every year.

Woodson returned for the 2011 season, fit and ready to mentor the young members of the team, his desire for them to become top notch players. He wanted to assist them in running their routes with expertise. He also wanted them to realize that each one carries the other. Without one mind, one goal, one purpose, and one heart, they would not become who they wanted to be. Being united made them a team able to overcome adversity.

Woodson's statement speaks to the heart of the Christian life. Commitment to the Lord, to the Bible, and to each other is what Jesus taught. Are we giving our best to the Lord and to those around us? Jesus laid down His life in the ultimate commitment for all of mankind. He walked with one mind, one goal, one purpose, and one heart with God, and He did all that for you and me.

Let's give Him our minds, goals, purposes, and hearts for His glory.

EXTRA POINT:

Lord, I want to give you my mind, goals, purposes, and heart, because You first gave me Yours.

Follow the Anointing

Deuteronomy 28:1-14

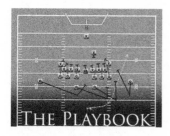

THE PLAYBOOK

FROM THE PLAYBOOK:

Blessed shall you be when you come in, and blessed shall you be when you go out.

Deuteronomy 28:6

"**I**f I did what I was supposed to do, which is stay in the end zone like my coach told me, y'all probably wouldn't know my name right now."[50] Instead, Randall Cobb moved from eight yards deep in the end zone, midway through the third quarter, and took the ball all the way to the other end zone. Not only did he help the Packers win the season opener against the New Orleans Saints, Super Bowl winners of the 2009 season, but he gained the honor of National Football League Play of the Year.

Cobb said he could barely make his Lambeau leap, he was so winded, and he needed oxygen when he returned to the sideline.

Cobb received the award at the National Football League's Night of Honor, two evenings before the Super Bowl, in February, 2012, where Aaron Rodgers won the Most Valuable Player award for the season.[51]

Had there been an award for Best Assist to the Play of the Year, it would have gone to John Kuhn, the Packer running back who was in his seventh season. Kuhn was covering the New Orleans Saint who hit Cobb shortly out of the end zone between the 20- and 25-yard lines. Cobb bounced off the man right into Kuhn and was about to go down. Kuhn held him up so only Cobb's hand touched the ground, and then Kuhn actually turned him around and pointed him in the right direction.[52] Cobb continued to the Lambeau leaping, oxygen draining, NFL Play of the Year award. The score went from 28-20 to 35-20.

Are you the kid who takes chances when your boss says to play it safe, because he knows you sometimes cough up the ball? Or are you the veteran who does his job and keeps the kid moving so he can be recognized and awarded? Maybe you're the boss who clenches his teeth, then chuckles and cheers as his team pulls off the Play of the Year.

We've all probably played one of those roles. The important thing is that we help the team by adjusting to the situation without knowing the outcome.

Randall Cobb didn't always have good results with his impetuousness. John Kuhn wasn't always in the right place at the right time, even though he usually is. And, Mike McCarthy, whose coaching takes a back seat to no one, readily admits that he doesn't always give the best advice.

So, how do we make sure we are where we should be and doing what we should do, whether it is to grab the opportunity or kneel on the ball? We must learn to listen to the Holy Spirit. We can train our hearts and minds to yield to the truth of the Bible and the leading of God's voice within. It is a daily training, just like football, except there is no off season.

Many find it best to start early in the day, reading or listening to the Bible. As you believe what it says, it will begin to speak to you. You'll hear a thought: Do this, don't do this, do it now, wait. A scripture verse will float through your being at the oddest time and it will seem uncanny how it applies to the very situation you are in. That's God.

As a result of following those leads, you'll make a fantastic play or help it along or get credit for being the marvelous coach that you are. We need to learn, train, follow, and obey.

EXTRA POINT:

Lord, I choose to listen and obey as I seek You daily. Help me to learn to hear Your voice.

Endnotes

1   Pete Dougherty, "Soft Sell Lured White to Visit, Join Packers," *Green Bay Press Gazette*, December 27, 2004.

2   Greg Jennings with Pam Oliver, "Super Bowl XLV," Fox Sports. WLUK FOX 11, Green Bay, February 6, 2011.

3   @GregJennings. "To whom much is given much is given, of him much is required" Luke 12:48. Thank you Lord for giving me this opportunity to #BeGreat today!!!" Twitter.com. 15 Jan. 2012, 11:57 a.m. Tweet.

4   Mike Vandermause, "Parallels for 1962, 2011 seasons run straight to high-stakes Thanksgiving games," Packersnews. com, November 22, 2011, http://pqasb.pqarchiver.com/ greenbaypressgazette/access/2518784231.html.

5   Tramon Williams, interview by Larry McCarren, Larry McCarren's Locker Room Show, WFRV, Green Bay, December 20, 2010.

6   mysticfish, "Mr. Rogers Neighborhood," MYSTIC WATERS. com Fly Fishing Blog, December 9, 2011, mysticwaters.com/ blog/2011/12/09/mr-rogers-neighborhood.

7   Kareem Copeland, "Rodgers Reigns as MVP," *Green Bay Press Gazette*, February 5, 2012.

8   Ibid.

9   Steven Sullivan, "Sully Says (Role Models)," KATV, ABC, April 9, 2012.

10 John Kuhn, interview by Larry McCarren, Larry McCarren's Locker Room Show, WFRV, Green Bay, December 5, 2011.

11 "Bio," The Official Website of Brett Favre, www.officialbrettfavre. com/bio (August 8, 2012).

12 ABC (Producer). (2007, December 21). MNF Story on Favre After His Dad Died [Video file]. Retrieved from http://www. youtube.com/watch?v=gZV0WFKUt2k.

13 Mike Florio, "Jermichael Finley carted off with injury," Profootballtalk.nbcsports.com, October 10, 2010, http://profootballtalk.nbcsports.com/2010/10/10/ jermichael-finley-carted-off-with-injury/.

14 Rylin Media, LLC, 4-Pack! The Green Bay Packers Bring Super Bowl Title Number Four to Titletown USA! (Willowbrook: Rylin Media, 2011), 92.

15 Charles Davis, "Pittsburgh Steelers Fans Trash Talk During Friday Rally," Green Bay Press Gazette, January 29, 2011.

16 "Real Purpose," Facing the Giants, Directed by Alex Kendrick (2006; Sony Home Entertainment, 2007), DVD.

17 Pete Dougherty, "Packers 23, Vikings 20," Green Bay Press Gazette, September 26, 1999.

18 Jim Polzin, "Super Bowl XLV: Driver's game-ending injury can't spoil 'blessing' of long-awaited title," February 7, 2011, http://host.madison.com/sports/football/professional/ super-bowl-xlv-driver-s-game-ending-injury-can-t/ article_2f5b406c-328c-11e0-9e8b-001cc4c03286.html.

19 James Jones, interview by Larry McCarren, Mike McCarthy Show, WFRV, Green Bay, January 17, 2012.

20 White, Reggie. In The Trenches: The Autobiography. With Jim Denney. Nashville: Thomas Nelson, Inc., 1996, 1997, 185.

21 Ibid, 187.

22 "Larry McCarren Biography," Packers Hall of Fame, http:// larrymccarren.packershalloffame.com/biography/ (August 8, 2012).

23 Brett Favre and Bonita Favre. Favre. With Chris Havel. New York

City: Rugged Land, LLC, 2004.

24 Jen Lada, "Save Me a Spot," July, 21, 2010, http://community. fox6now.com/_Save-Me-a-Spot/blog/2346141/95548.html (dead link).

25 Jason Cole, "Rodgers hides Packers' flaws in pursuit of 16-0," December 5, 2011, http://sports.yahoo.com/nfl/news?slug=jc-cole_aaron_rodgers_green_bay_packers_giants120411.

26 Dinesh Ramde, "Football fans get a chance to buy stock in Green Bay Packers," Assoicated Press, December 2, 2011, http://www.usatoday.com/money/perfi/stocks/story/2011-12-02/green-bay-packers-stock-sale/51587896/1.

27 Kevin Seifert, "Obama: Can Bears have Aaron Rodgers?" August 12, 2011, http://espn.go.com/blog/nflnation/post/_/id/43288/obama-can-bears-have-aaron-rodgers.

28 Chariots of Fire, Directed by Hugh Hudson, (1981; 20th Century Fox)

29 Lori Nickel, "Packers' Matthews has football in his blood," Journal Sentinel, November 7, 2010, http://www.jsonline.com/sports/packers/106834678.html.

30 Michael David Smith, "Clay Matthews' hit was the play of the game," February 6, 2011, http://profootballtalk.nbcsports.com/2011/02/06/clay-matthews-hit-was-the-play-of-the-game/.

31 Kevin Seifert, "Lockout tweets by @espn_nfcnblog," July 27, 2011, http://www.twylah.com/espn_nfcnblog/tweets/96041970329325570.

32 Rylin Media, LLC, 4-Pack! The Green Bay Packers Bring Super Bowl Title Number Four to Titletown USA! (Willowbrook: Rylin Media, 2011), 98.

33 Rob Demovsky, "In Two Seasons Packers Go From Worst to First," Green Bay Press Gazette Packers Preview, December 31, 2011.

34 Ibid.

35 Ibid.

36 Kevin Seifert, "Autopsy: Michael Philbin drowned," The Associated Press, January 11, 2012, http://espn.go.com/new-york/nfl/story/_/id/7450845/autopsy-green-bay-packers-coach-joe-philbin-son-michael-philbin-drowned.

37 "The Packers' Season in Review," Green Bay Press Gazette, January 29, 2012.

38 Rick Reilly, "I believe in Tim Tebow," January 13, 2012, http://espn.go.com/espn/story/_/id/7455943/believing-tim-tebow.

39 Steve Rose, Leap of Faith: God Must Be a Packer Fan, (Neshkoro: Angel Press of WI, 1996), 30.

40 Ibid, 29.

41 Ibid, 19.

42 Rob Reischel, "Merry Christmas," 100 Things Packer Fans Should Know & Do Before They Die, (Chicago: Triumph Books, 2010), 238-239.

43 Scott Wells, interview by Larry McCarren, Larry McCarren's Locker Room Show, WFRV, Green Bay, December 27, 2011.

44 Ibid.

45 Rob Demovsky, "Green Bay Packers, Chicago Bears won't pull any punches on Sunday," January 19, 2011, http://www.packersnews.com/article/20110119/PKR01/110119153/-We-need-to-knock-them-out-No-pulled-punches-planned-for-Sunday.

46 Rylin Media, LLC, 4-Pack! The Green Bay Packers Bring Super Bowl Title Number Four to Titletown USA! (Willowbrook: Rylin Media, 2011), 86-88.

47 Jason Wilde, "Woodson's approach: Follow the leader," August 21, 2011, http://www.espnmilwaukee.com/corp/page/08%2F20%2F11_Woodson%27s_approach:_Follow_the_leader/89?feed=2&utm_source=twitterfeed&utm_medium=twitter.

48 Bob McGinn, "Is Hall of Fame within Woodson's reach?" Journal

Sentinel, August 12, 2011, http://www.jsonline.com/sports/packers/127628733.html.

49 Jim Polzin, "Woodson becoming voice of the Packers," Portage Daily Register, January 26, 2011, http://www.wiscnews.com/portagedailyregister/sports/football/professional/article_c51e8dd4-29cc-11e0-8e15-001cc4c002e0.html.

50 "NFL Honors," NBC26, WGBA, Green Bay, February 4, 2012.

51 Ibid.

52 John Kuhn, interview by Larry McCarren, Larry McCarren's Locker Room Show, WFRV, Green Bay, December 5, 2011.

Made in the USA
Coppell, TX
07 October 2021

63616497R00069